Let's Make a Picture Graph

by Robin Nelson

first step nonfiction

Lerner Publications Company · Minneapolis

Dan, Emma, and Ron
picked apples.

They wanted to show how
many apples they picked.

Apples Picked

Dan	🍎🍎🍎🍎🍎🍎🍎
Emma	🍎🍎🍎
Ron	🍎🍎🍎🍎🍎🍎🍎🍎

They used a **picture graph**. It uses pictures to show information.

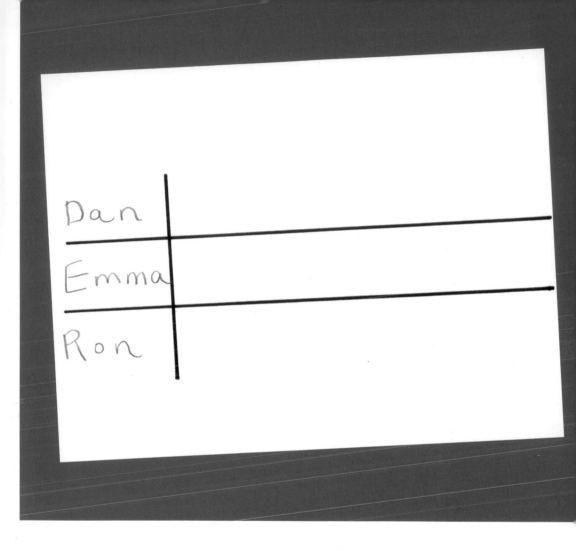

They wrote their names on
the side of their graph.

They counted the apples
they each picked.

Apples Picked

Dan   7

Emma   3

Ron   8

The numbers are their **data**.

Dan picked seven apples.

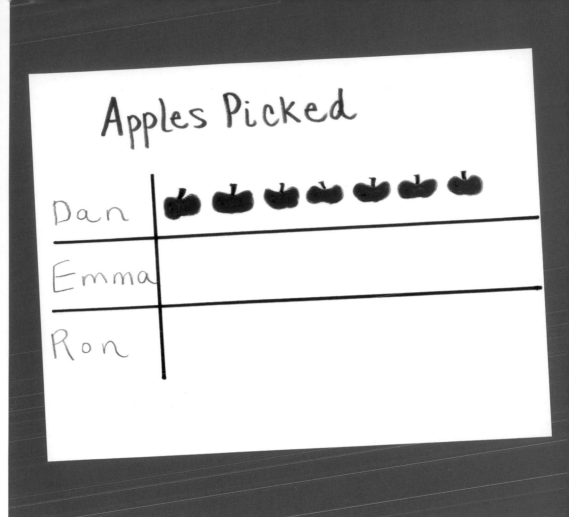

He drew seven apples after his name.

Emma picked three apples.

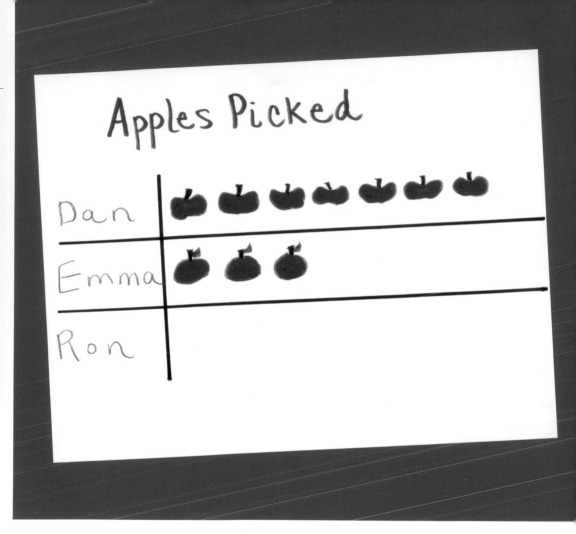

She drew three apples after her name.

Ron picked eight apples.

He drew eight apples after his name.

Emma picked four fewer
apples than Dan.

Ron picked five more
apples than Emma.

Emma picked the least
apples.

Ron picked the most apples.

Apples Picked

Dan	🍎🍎🍎🍎🍎🍎🍎
Emma	🍎🍎🍎
Ron	🍎🍎🍎🍎🍎🍎🍎🍎

The Same Number of Apples

Dan, Emma, and Ron want to have the same number of apples.

How many apples should Dan give to Emma?

How many apples should Ron give to Emma?

How many apples will each friend have if they each have the same number?

How to Make a Picture Graph

 Decide what information you want to graph.

 Label the bottom or side of your picture graph.

 Count to get your data.

 Use your data to draw your pictures.

 Add a title.

Kinds of Days

Cloudy	☁	☁	☁
rainy	🌧	🌧	
Sunny	☀	☀	☀ ☀

Glossary

 data – information used to create a graph

 label – to write words on a graph that tell about the data

 picture graph – a graph that shows information using pictures

LERNER e SOURCE

Expand learning beyond the printed book. Download free, complementary educational resources for this book from our website, www.lerneresource.com.

Index

apples – 2–3, 6, 8–17

counted – 6

data – 7

pictures – 4

The images in this book are used with the permission of: © Gabe Palacio/Aurora/Getty Images, pp. 2 (left), 3; © AAGAMIA/Iconica/Getty Images, pp. 2 (center), 10, 16; Nick Dolding/Cultura/Newscom, pp. 2 (right), 12, 17; © Todd Strand/Independent Picture Service, pp. 4, 5, 7, 9, 11, 13, 14, 15, 18, 20, 21, 22; © Yuris Schulz/Shutterstock.com, p. 6; © mareandmare/Shutterstock.com, p. 8.

Front cover: © Jon Fischer/Independent Picture Service.

Main body text set in ITC Avant Garde Gothic Std Medium 21/25.
Typeface provided by Adobe Systems

Lerner Publications Company
A division of Lerner Publishing Group, Inc.
241 First Avenue North
Minneapolis, MN 55401 U.S.A.

Website address: www.lernerbooks.com

Library of Congress Cataloging-in-Publication Data

Nelson, Robin, 1971–
    Let's make a picture graph / by Robin Nelson.
        p.   cm. — (First step nonfiction - graph it!)
    Includes index.
    ISBN 978–0–7613–8973–6 (lib. bdg. : alk. paper)
    1. Mathematical statistics—Graphic methods—Juvenile literature. I. Title.
QA276.13.N45 2013
001.4'226—dc23   2011044697

Manufactured in the United States of America
1 – BC – 7/15/12